SOUTH AMERICA

A TRUE BOOK

by
David Petersen

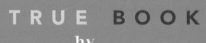

Children's Press®
A Division of Grolier Publishing

New York London Hong Kong Sydney
Danbury, Connecticut

A victoria
regia lily pad

Reading Consultant
Linda Cornwell
Learning Resource Consultant
Indiana Department of
Education

Visit Children's Press on the Internet at:
http://publishing.grolier.com

Library of Congress Cataloging-in-Publication Data

Petersen, David, 1946–
    South America / by David Petersen.
        p.   cm. — (A true book)
    Includes bibliographical references and index.
    Summary: Introduces the geography, history, climate, and culture of
South America.
    ISBN 0-516-20769-5 (lib.bdg.)   0-516-26440-0 (pbk.)
    1. South America—Description and travel—Juvenile literature.
[1. South America.] I. Title. II. Series.
F2264.2.P48   1998
968—dc21   98-24338
                                                               CIP
                                                               AC

Contents

CENTRAL
AMERICA

Caribbean Sea

L. Maracaibo

Panama Canal

Caracas

VENEZUELA

GUYANA

SURINAME

Georgetown

Paramaribo

FR. GUIANA

Cayenne

NORTH
ATLANTIC
OCEAN

Bogotá

LLANOS

COLOMBIA

Equator

Quito

ECUADOR

Amazon River

PERU

SELVAS

BRAZIL

Lima

ANDES MOUNTAINS

L. Titicaca

La Paz

BOLIVIA

Sucre

Brasília

BRAZILIAN
HIGHLANDS

Atacama
Desert

Tropic of Capricorn

PARAGUAY

São Paulo

Rio de Janiero

Iguaçu Falls

CHILE

Asunción

GRAN CHACO

ARGENTINA

Mt. Aconcagua

SOUTH
ATLANTIC
OCEAN

Santiago

SOUTH
PACIFIC
OCEAN

URUGUAY

Buenos Aires

Montevideo

PAMPAS

Falkland I. (Br.)

Drake Passage

Tierro del Fuego

Cape Horn

SOUTH
AMERICA

● Capital city

0   600 Miles

0   900 Kilometers

A Land of Diversity

If Earth's seven continents were lined up according to their size, South America would stand in the middle. It's larger than Australia, Europe, and Antarctica, but smaller than Asia, Africa, and North America. Its shape is roughly triangular—widest at the top, narrowing to a point at the bottom.

"South" America actually lies southeast of North America. South and North America are joined by a narrow strip of land called the Isthmus of Panama. Without that slender land connection, South America would be Earth's largest island. The continent is almost completely surrounded by water. The Caribbean Sea is on the north,

Magellanic penguins on
the beaches of Patagonia

the Atlantic Ocean on the
east, the Pacific Ocean on the
west, and the Drake Passage
lies to the south.

The Drake Passage is a sea-
way that separates South
America from frozen Antarctica,

600 miles (970 kilometers) farther south. These southern regions of South America are home to such cold-loving creatures as penguins and fur seals.

Yet, strange as it seems, South America also contains the world's largest jungle. Jungles, or tropical rain forests, are always warm, wet, green, and near the equator.

Equatorial regions get more sunlight than anywhere else on Earth, and they have no winter

Rain forests are always warm and wet.

at all. In addition to heat, the abundant sunlight also promotes plant growth. If you add rain, which is plentiful near the equator, you have

The Amazon River is often called the Mar Dulce, meaning "freshwater sea."

the main ingredients for a tropical rain forest.

In South America, the rain forest is called the Selva. Its lifeline is the Amazon River.

Do You Know About the Equator?

Imagine Earth as a basketball. If you poked a stick into the top of the ball, down through its center, and out the bottom, the stick would represent the globe's axis. The Earth completes one spin daily on its axis.

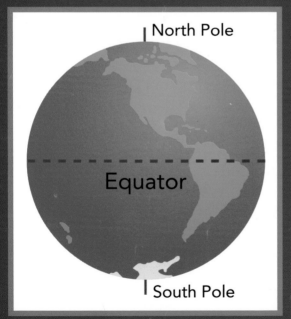

North Pole

Equator

South Pole

The point where the stick enters the top of the ball represents the North Pole. The point where the stick exits from the bottom of the ball is the South Pole. Now if you were to draw a line, like a belt, around the middle of the ball, midway between the two poles—that belt would be the equator.

The Mighty Amazon

Look at a map of South America, and you'll see that the equator crosses the top part of the continent, passing through Ecuador and Brazil. Just below the equator flows the mighty Amazon River.

Stretching for 4,000 miles (6,437 km), the Amazon is the

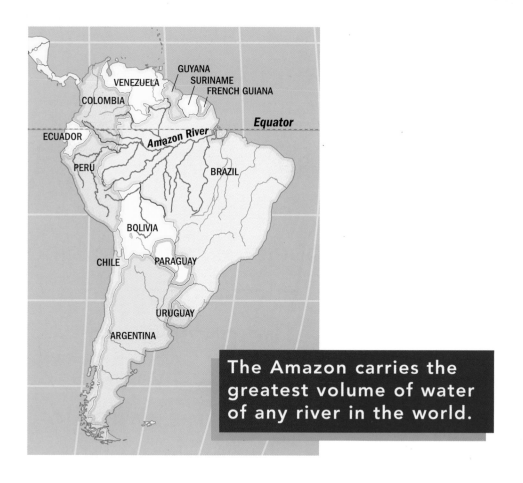

COLOMBIA
VENEZUELA
GUYANA
SURINAME
FRENCH GUIANA
ECUADOR
Equator
Amazon River
PERU
BRAZIL
BOLIVIA
CHILE
PARAGUAY
URUGUAY
ARGENTINA

The Amazon carries the greatest volume of water of any river in the world.

world's second-longest river. Only the Nile River in Africa is longer, but the Amazon carries much more water than the Nile.

More than two hundred kinds of fish live in the Amazon, including such interesting species as air-breathing lungfish, electric eels, and piranhas. The perch-sized piranha has wickedly sharp teeth. It sometimes swims in schools and eagerly attacks larger animals.

Many kinds of monkeys swing through the treetops of the Selva. Their noisy neighbors in the forest canopy

The Selva is home to many creatures such as the red-bellied piranha (top left), emperor tamarin monkey (top right), and the red-crowned parrot (left).

include big-billed toucans, colorful parrots and macaws, and other species far too numerous to list.

The most majestic Selva creature is the jaguar, the Americas' largest wildcat. Jaguars have black spots on their golden fur, and big, haunting eyes. They live by hunting meaty jungle residents, such as monkeys and tapirs—(hooved mammals that look a lot like pigs).

Jaguars can weigh up to 400 pounds (180 kilograms).

Another leading member of the Amazon wildlife community is the anaconda, one of the world's largest snakes. These shy reptiles grow 30 feet (9 meters) or more in length.

Save the Rain Forests!

Some areas of the jungle have been destroyed for gold mining

The Selva of South America contains more species of plants than any other region on Earth. Here you will find a spectacular array of wild orchids, and more than 2,500 kinds of trees. Many medicines and other important products come from rain forest plants. This great, green tangle of life also produces much of the Earth's oxygen.

Sadly, the rain forest is being logged, strip-mined, burned, ranched, settled, and otherwise destroyed. And with the loss of the rain forest, Earth loses countless plant and animal species forever.

The Awesome Andes

West of the Selva rise the awesome Andes, the world's longest mountain range. The Andes stretch 4,500 miles (7,200 km) along South America's Pacific coast.

The Andes are the second-highest mountains in the world. Only the Himalaya, in

A view of the Andes Mountains in Chile (left) and Mount Aconcagua (below)

Asia, are higher. Many snow-capped Andean peaks rise more than 20,000 feet (6,100 m) above sea level. The tallest of all is Mount Aconcagua in Argentina. Aconcagua soars 22,831 feet (6,959 m) above the nearby Pacific Ocean.

Entirely at home in this lofty habitat are two wild relatives of the camel—the vicuña and the guanaco. Two important domestic animals, the alpaca and the llama, are

A llama

descended from the guana-
co. People use llamas as pack
animals, while alpacas pro-
duce the world's finest wool.
The Andes are also home
to the world's largest flying

The Andean condor is the world's largest flying bird.

bird, the Andean condor. This huge scavenger has a wingspan of about 10 feet (3 m). It glides gracefully for long distances, flapping its wings only once an hour.

The Atacama Desert is one of the driest regions in the world.

Nestled between the Andes Mountains and the Pacific coast is the Atacama Desert— the driest place on earth. From the highest mountains to the driest deserts, South America truly is a land of great natural diversity.

24

The Great Central Plains

Looking from west to east, South America has three distinct geographical features. Along the western edge of the continent stand the Andes Mountains. The east has the Eastern Highlands of Brazil and Guiana. And between these two mountainous areas sprawl the vast Central Plains.

A view of South
America from high
above the earth

The Central Plains can be
divided into four regions,
north to south. The north—
Columbia and Venezuela—
has an expanse of rolling

plains called the Llanos.
Water and grass are plentiful
here, and cattle ranching is
the primary industry.

The Llanos cover more than 100,000
square miles (260,000 sq. km).

South of the Llanos, the lush, wet jungle of the Selva carpets the continent in bright green. The Selva runs along the equator in Peru, Brazil, and Bolivia.

Farther south lie the hardwood scrub forests—the Gran Chaco of Bolivia, Paraguay, and Argentina. This is the hottest part of the continent, where summer temperatures climb as high as 110 degrees Fahrenheit (43 degrees Celsius).

South America's fertile plains are rich ground for farming or for cattle grazing.

The southernmost region of the Central Plains are the vast grasslands of the Argentine Pampa, with rich fertile soil for farming and plenty of grass for sheep and cattle grazing.

Patagonia (above) comes from the Spanish word *patagones* meaning "big feet."

South of the Central Plains and far from the warming equator lies the cool, dry Patagonian plateau. The flightless, ostrich-like rhea is found here. It is the largest bird in the Americas.

Of South America's many off-shore islands, the most interesting are the Galápagos Islands. Here, 600 miles (970 km) off the Pacific coast of Ecuador, live many unusual species of wildlife. You may know about the giant Galápagos turtle, which weighs more than 500 pounds (230 km) and can live for a hundred years.

The giant Galápagos turtle is one of the world's oldest living creatures.

Watery Wonders

South America's largest lake is Maracaibo in Venezuela, covering 5,217 square miles (13,512 sq. km). Perched at 12,507 feet (3,812 m) in the Andes, on the border between Peru and Bolivia, is jewel-like Lake Titicaca—the world's highest navigable lake.

Lake Titicaca (above) is 12,507 feet (3,812 m) above sea level. An aerial view of Angel Falls in Venezuela (right).

With so many rivers and mountains, South America has some of the world's most spectacular waterfalls. The highest is Angel Falls in Venezuela, which plunges more than a half-mile straight down.

The Iguaçu Falls are a favorite tourist attraction in Brazil and Argentina.

Equally impressive is Iguaçu Falls, on the border between Brazil and Argentina. Iguaçu is about as high as a 23-story building, and it forms a thunderous wall of water 2 miles (3.2 km) wide!

The People of South America

The native peoples of South America are Indians whose ancestors arrived at least 11,000 years ago, and possibly much earlier. Until the early 1900s, most South American Indians lived like their ancestors—hunting, fishing, gathering wild plants, and growing

Many Indians in South America still practice the traditions of their ancestors.

small gardens. In the most remote parts of the Selva, a few small tribes still follow this simple way of life.

One of the first groups of South American Indians to

give up the nomadic life of hunting and gathering were the Incas of the Andes Mountains and northern Pacific Coast. Hundreds of years ago, the Incas settled down to become farmers and went on to build great stone cities, create art in gold and gemstones, and rule a power-ful empire. At dozens of archaeological sites, such as Machu Picchu in the Peruvian Andes, magnificent Inca cities

This Inca village in Machu Picchu was abandoned after the Spaniards overthrew the Inca empire in the 1500s.

still stand proudly today. But the once-mighty Inca empire is long dead.

In the 16th century, the Spanish arrived from Europe. In no time, the Inca civilization was destroyed and its fabulous riches were stolen by the Spaniards. The Inca population-shrank from diseases brought by the Europeans, as well as the cruelty of the Spanish invaders.

Francisco Pizarro (center) ordered Incan ruler Atahualpa (left) to be killed shortly after this meeting in 1533.

All over South America, other native people suffered similar disasters. Even so, Indians still make up the majority of South America's population today. Many have mixed Indian and European or African ancestry.

In remote areas, traditional native languages are still spoken. But in the cities, where 75 percent of South America's 323 million people live, most people speak Spanish. The

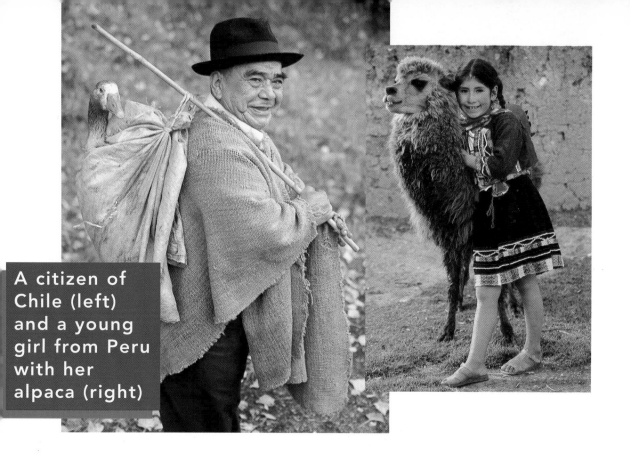

exception is Brazil, where Portuguese is spoken.

While modern South America has several large, bustling cities and coastal tourist centers, the continent's real

One of the most famous sights in South America is the statue of Christ the Redeemer. Standing over 124 feet tall (38m), high above the city of Rio de Janeiro, Catholic worshipers believe the statue blesses the many citizens of Brazil.

beauty is in the spectacular diversity of its natural wonders—in the jungles, rivers, lakes, waterfalls, and wildlife, and in its native peoples. When you visit South America, these are the sights to see.

South America Fast Facts

Area 6,885,000 square miles (17,833,000 sq. km)

Coastline 20,000 miles (32,000 km)

Highest point Aconcagua Peak, Argentina: 22,831 feet (6,959 m) above sea level

Highest waterfall Angel Falls, Venezuela: 3,212 feet (979 m)

Largest lake Maracaibo, Venezuela: 5,217 square miles (13,512 sq. km)

Longest river Amazon: 4,000 miles (6,437 km)

Lowest point Valdés Peninsula, Argentina: 131 feet (40 m) below sea level

Number of independent nations 12

Population 323 million (1996 estimates)

To Find Out More

Here are some additional resources to help you learn more about the continent of South America:

 **Books**

Planet Earth: World Geography. Oxford University Press, 1993.

Blue, Rose and Corinne Naden. **Andes Mountains.** Raintree Steck-Vaughn, 1994.

Heinrichs, Ann. **Venezuela.** Children's Press, 1997.

Jackson, Alys. **Plains Indians.** Viking Children's Books, 1997.

Myers, Christopher and Lynne. **Galapagos: Islands of Change.** Hyperion Books for Children, 1995.

Reynolds, Jan. **Amazon Basin.** Harcourt Brace, 1993.

Savage, Steven. **Animals of the Rain Forest.** Raintree Steck-Vaughn, 1997.

Steele, Philip. **Incas & Machu Picchu.** Silver Burdett Press, 1993.

Organizations and Online Sites

Explore More Projects for South American Studies
http://www.ospi.wednet. edu:8001/curric/weather/ adptcty/projsugg.html

Learn more about the geography, people, and culture of South America while participating in fun projects designed especially for students.

INTELLICast: USA Weather
http://www.intellicast.com/ weather/intl/hisasat/

Forecasts and weather information for South America and other continents around the globe.

NOVA/ Ice Mummies of the Inca
http://www.pbs.org/wgbh/ nova/peru/

Journey to the high Andes Mountains with a team of archaeologists to unearth frozen mummies from five hundred years ago.

South America Cybertour
http://www.wp.com/ virtualvoyager/

This page takes you on a "Cybertour" of South America in seconds! Updated with exciting information, photos, Quicktime movies, and RealAudio sound clips.

Venezuelan Amazon Expedition
http://sunsite.doc.ic.ac.uk/ netspedition/amazon.html

Take a journey along the Amazon, including photos, maps, and wildlife.

Important Words

archaeology the study of the physical remains of ancient human cultures

axis the imaginary line around which the earth spins

canopy a protective covering, such as the leafy treetops of a rain forest

geography the study of the earth's surface features, such as continents, oceans, and mountains

habitat the place and natural conditions in which a plant or an animal lives

navigable a body of water wide and deep enough to carry ships

nomad a person who frequently moves, having no permanent home

scavenger an animal or bird that feeds on the remains of dead animals

school a group of fish or other sea creatures swimming together

Index

Meet the Author

David Petersen writes about nature and the world. His most recent book is *The Nearby Faraway: A Personal Journey through the Heart of the West* (Johnson Books).

He has written dozens of books for Children's Press, including True Books on national parks and all the continents of the world. David lives in a cabin on a mountain in Colorado. He likes to read, write, walk with his dogs in the woods, camp, hunt, fish, and explore the world.